COMING TO AMERICA

THROUGH THE ANGEL ISLAND IMMIGRATION STATION

A HISTORY SEEKING ADVENTURE

by Ailynn Collins

CAPSTONE PRESS
a capstone imprint

Published by You Choose, an imprint of Capstone
1710 Roe Crest Drive, North Mankato, Minnesota 56003
capstonepub.com

Library of Congress Cataloging-in-Publication Data is available on the Library of
Congress website.

ISBN: 9781669032557 (hardcover)
ISBN: 9781669032724 (paperback)
ISBN: 9781669032663 (ebook PDF)

Summary: YOU are an Asian immigrant in the early 1900s. You dream of a life
in American, but first you'll have to pass through the Angel Island Immigration
Station. How long will you be stuck there? And will you pass the necessary tests or
be sent back? Step back in time to face the challenges and decisions that real people
encountered as they sought a better life in a different country.

Editorial Credits
Editor: Mandy Robbins; Designer: Heidi Thompson; Media Researcher: Jo Miller;
Production Specialist: Tori Abraham

Image Credits
Alamy: Chronicle, 46, Imago History Collection, 82, Niday Picture Library, 10,
North Wind Picture Archives, 25; Associated Press, 64; Getty Images: Bettmann,
52; North Wind Picture Archives via AP Images, 103; Science Source: National
Archives and Records Administration, 32; Shutterstock: Everett Collection, Cover,
7, Roman Debree, 36, spinetta, 92, vladm, 70; The Jon B. Lovelace Collection
of California Photographs in Carol M. Highsmith's America Project, Library of
Congress, Prints and Photographs Division, 40, 76; Wikimedia: Hawaii State
Archives, 89, NARA, 29, 49, The Bancroft Library, University of California,
Berkeley, 4, US Government, 105; Wikipedia: NPS, 58

All internet sites appearing in back matter were available and accurate when this
book was sent to press.

TABLE OF CONTENTS

ABOUT YOUR ADVENTURE

YOU are an Asian immigrant in the early 1900s, hoping for a better life in the United States. Many people from your homeland are struggling and looking for opportunities to improve their lives by moving to the United States.

But it's not as easy for people from Asian countries as it is for people from Europe. Before you can create a new life in the United States, you must make your way through the Angel Island Immigration Station.

Turn the page.

The requirements for entering this new country are more difficult for Asian immigrants than for white immigrants, especially the Chinese. Racist laws have been put in place to keep as many Asians out of the country as possible.

Do you have the skill—and the luck—to make your way into America? YOU CHOOSE which paths to take. Will you risk it all or play it safe? Will you survive and thrive, or will your dreams be shattered?

Turn the page to begin your adventure.

Angel Island Immigration Station, 1901

CHAPTER 1

A GOLDEN OPPORTUNITY

The 1900s are just beginning. Life is difficult in countries such as China, Japan, and Korea. Wars in these places threaten people's safety, especially the poor. Farmers' crops are failing due to flooding.

Families are starving. Often, the only food you have to eat is soggy rice with a bit of salt. You see no hope in sight if you stay in your homeland.

Turn the page.

A family in a fishing village in China

You and your fellow villagers have heard of a place in the western part of the United States called the Gold Mountain. For many years now, men have left their families to travel to America.

At first, men went to Gold Mountain to find gold. When the gold ran out, they went there to find jobs that paid better than anything in their homelands. When they come home, they bring gifts and wear fine clothes. They have clearly earned enough money to support their families.

Some men return to take a wife. Others send for a wife. The brides often stay behind for a time. They receive money from their husbands in America. Some of these women travel with their husbands to the Gold Mountain. Most are sent for and meet their husbands in this strange new land.

Turn the page.

Going to America may be the only way you can save yourself and your family. You will have to leave everything you know and go to a faraway land where they speak a different language.

Will you be able to make it to Gold Mountain?

- To be a boy whose father wants to take him to America, turn to page 15.

- To journey to America as a young bride, turn to page 45.

- To head out as a young man with his wife, turn to page 75.

CHAPTER 2

JOURNEY TO GOLD MOUNTAIN

Your father was born in America, but his parents were Chinese. He returns to China every few years. First, it was to marry and then to start a family. You've only met him four times. New American laws against Chinese immigrants make it difficult for your family to move there with him.

His most recent three-month visit is coming to an end, and he has announced that he is planning to take you back with him. Ever since then, you've been having nightmares.

Turn the page.

You don't want to leave your mother and two sisters. You know that if it wasn't for the money Father sends from America, your whole family would starve. You are grateful, but he is practically a stranger. You don't want to go with him.

Mother says at 12 years old, you're nearly a man. Dare you disobey your parents and hide until Father leaves?

• To run away and hide, go to the next page.
• To do as you're told, turn to page 22.

You run to your best friend's house and beg him to hide you.

He helps you into a woven basket with a lid. "We used to keep rice in there," he says. "It's been empty for so long, no one will look inside."

You climb into the basket and pull the lid shut. After several hours, your legs cramp up. You think the house is empty, so you stand up to stretch. That's when you hear your friend's mother.

"I found him!" she shrieks.

She drags you to the village center. Everyone gathers. Father has his arms crossed over his chest. Mother is crying.

"You could've delayed your father's journey," Mother scolds. "What were you thinking?"

Turn the page.

"Such bad behavior!" Father's voice booms. "Maybe you'll be too much trouble in America."

You are too scared to speak.

"Why wouldn't you want to go to Gold Mountain?" a neighbor asks. "Look at how successful your father has been."

"Your father has kept our village from starvation," an uncle says. "Surely, you'd want to help him."

An old woman called Grannie May steps forward. A teenage boy helps her walk.

In a quivering voice, she speaks. "This is my great nephew, Soong. He has no family left. If your son refuses to go, please take him as your paper son."

"You want him to pretend to be our son?" Mother gasps.

"That is dangerous," Father says. "If he fails the interrogations, he will be sent back. And I would be deported for lying."

"Better he tries than starve," she says. "He doesn't have a future here."

There's a long moment of silence as the entire village stares at you, your father, and Soong.

"I can only take one son," Father says. "Who shall it be?" he asks you.

You must decide. You don't want to let your family down. But leaving everything you've ever known is terrifying. Do you go with your father or let Soong go instead?

- To let Soong go in your place, turn to page 20.
- To go with Father to America, turn to page 22.

You want to stay with Mother and your sisters. You don't care if people think you're a coward. Over time, you will prove to the rest of the village that you will take care of your family in your own way. You will stay with the people you love.

Soong looks strong. He will probably be a better helper to Father anyway. And if he goes, Granny Mae will receive help too.

"You should take Soong," you say.

Your parents are disappointed, but Granny Mae is thrilled. Father says goodbye and takes Soong with him.

Life is difficult after Father is gone. The river overflows several times in the next few months. The farm fields flood, and there is barely enough food to feed the village. Everyone eagerly awaits the money sent by Father and Soong.

A few months later, Soong and Father return. Soong could not pass the interrogation, so both men were deported. Father is furious. He blames you. Now, your family will have to find a new way to make a living.

You feel like such a failure. All you had wanted was to stay with your family. Your wrong decision is now their downfall.

THE END

To follow another path, turn to page 12.
To learn more about the difficult history of Asians in America, turn to page 101.

It would be selfish of you to stay in China. Your entire village depends on men sending money from America.

"I'll come with you," you say.

You pack a bag with your few belongings. You catch a ride to the nearest city. From there, you take a train to the port. You get on a small boat to Hong Kong.

You spend four days in Hong Kong, waiting for the ship that will take you to America. There, Father buys you a new suit. You exchange your loose, knee-length pants and baggy shirt for a tight white shirt, a dark jacket, and matching pants. You even get a hat like Father's.

"Men who look healthy, clean, and wealthy are allowed through Angel Island more easily," Father explains. Then he hands you a packet of papers.

"You'll need to know the answers to questions about your home," he says. He hands you maps and other information about your village.

"I know everything here," you say. "I've lived there my whole life."

"How many chickens do our neighbors have?" Father asks.

You scratch your head.

"See? You don't know," Father continues. "Our answers must match so you don't fail the interrogations. When we arrive, we'll destroy the papers. The Americans cannot know you've been studying."

You pack the papers into your suitcase. You think of your family back home. They're depending on you to get the answers right.

Turn the page.

You board the biggest ship you've ever seen, called *China*. You and Father follow hundreds of people to the bottom of the ship in steerage, the cheapest way to sail. It's just a large room that stinks of sweat and pee, with mats on the floor for sleeping.

Once the ship sets sail, Father takes you up to the deck. You breathe in the salty sea air. Well-dressed people stroll about the deck above you.

"Can we go up there?" you ask.

"We don't have the money to go up there," he says.

Back in steerage, you and Father make up beds in a corner. You meet several men. Some are on their way back to America. Others are going for the first time.

Chinese immigrants in steerage

One young man, Chin, spends every second studying his papers.

"I'm a 'paper son,'" Chin tells you. "I have to pretend to be my uncle's son. I changed my name, and I must know everything about his house and village."

"Won't they know how many children your uncle has already?" you ask.

"A long time ago, there was an earthquake in a city called San Francisco," Chin says. "All the citizenship records of the Chinese were destroyed, so we hope to get by with lying."

"I'm Father's real son. I shouldn't have a problem then," you say.

Chin smiles. "Just don't be nervous and make a mistake. They might think you're lying and send you back to China."

Chin's advice to not be nervous has the opposite effect on you. Now you're even more anxious than before about getting into America. What if the people there don't believe you're Father's son?

After three weeks, you arrive in America. You're very nervous. Father reminded you to destroy the papers, but you're afraid to let them go. You've heard it could take weeks before you are interrogated. What if you forget the answers?

- To throw away the papers, turn to page 28.
- To hide the papers in your clothes, turn to page 41.

You don't want to be turned away because you've been caught studying. You rip up the papers and throw them overboard. Then you hurry to your father's side.

The deck is packed with people. White men in suits and big hats come aboard to the upper deck.

"Those men are checking papers," Father says. "Passengers returning to their homeland can go to the city immediately."

"You were born here," you say. "Shouldn't you be allowed off?"

Father shakes his head. "This rule doesn't apply to most Chinese."

Soon, the men direct you and the rest of the passengers to a smaller boat.

Asian immigrants being inspected on the ferry to Angel Island

"This is the ferry to Angel Island," Father explains. "That's where we'll be interrogated."

In minutes, you step off the ferry onto a bridge leading to the white buildings on Angel Island. As everyone gets off, you hear many different languages. Father is silent, though. He looks nervous. This makes you nervous too.

Turn the page.

More white men approach. They separate the passengers into groups. Europeans are in one group. Japanese, Koreans, and other Asians are in another. The Chinese are separated into their own group. You wonder why your people are treated differently.

Your group walks past a white building to a smaller one behind it. These are the barracks where you'll stay. There are two stories. The women and small children go to a room on the ground floor. You follow the men to the upper level.

The large room is packed with rows of bunk beds, three-high. There's barely enough room to walk down the aisles. The windows have metal bars on them.

Father finds a spot near a window. You get the top bunk. The room smells like wet laundry.

"They're packing us in like farm animals," Chin says, taking the bunk next to yours.

You walk around and notice carvings on the walls. People have carved poems in Chinese. You stop to read a few. Some are sad. Others are angry.

In the evening, the men in your barracks are led to a large dining hall. The cooks serve an awful dinner. All the rice, vegetables, and mushy fruit are mixed together in one large bowl. It looks like the slop you fed the pigs back home. You swallow what you can.

The next day is even worse. The guards wake you early and take you to a big white building. All the Chinese men are placed in one room. No one knows what is about to happen.

Turn the page.

Young Asian immigrants being inspected on Angel Island

A bearded white man orders you to take off everything but your underpants. It's humiliating. Chinese people never remove their clothes in front of others.

It takes all day, but one-by-one, a doctor examines all the men. When it's your turn, the doctor inspects you. He says you're healthy.

Some men are immediately sent away. They look miserable.

"They failed their medical test," Father says. "They're going to the hospital. If they don't get better, they'll be sent back to China." You're not sure if you're jealous of those men or not

Every day on Angel Island is the same. In the morning, a guard calls out some names. Those men head out for their interrogations.

You eat twice a day in the dining room and spend the rest of the day in the barracks. Once a week, you're allowed into a small yard to get some sunshine.

After ten days, Father is called up for his interrogation. You wait nervously all day for him to return. Part of you is worried that he'll never come back.

Turn the page.

At the end of that day, the guard returns to announce the names of those who passed their tests. He calls out Father's name.

You turn to Father. His face is pale.

"Son, I must leave you here alone."

Your heart sinks. You don't want to be here without him. You feel like crying and clinging to Father.

- To allow yourself to feel upset, go to the next page.
- To hold your emotions in, turn to page 37.

You allow your tears to fall. Father tries to calm you. The guard frowns and approaches you.

"What is this about?" he demands.

"Please don't make me stay here alone," you cry. "I'm only twelve."

The guard laughs. "You Chinese are so spoiled. You're not the first boy to be separated from his family, and you won't be the last."

As he walks away, you beg him, "Please, sir! Can I do my interrogation now?"

He glares at you. "No. You can be quiet, or you will both be sent back to China." You run to your bunk and sob while Father is taken away.

Father visits you once a week and brings you dumplings. It's the only thing you look forward to.

Turn the page.

Chinese dumplings

He hides tiny pieces of paper in the shells of the peanuts that he brings you too. They are tips to help you when it's your turn for interrogation.

"Throw them away as soon as you've read them," he instructs. "These are some of the questions they asked me."

Life is almost unbearable. Finally, after a month, a guard calls your name.

• Go to page 38.

Father has to leave now. Making a fuss won't change that, so you do your best to be brave. Besides, you've gotten to know some of the other men here. You know at least a couple who will look out for you. And you want to impress Father with your bravery.

"I'll wait for you in San Francisco, and I'll visit in a week if you're not released by then," your father says.

"I'm sure it'll be my turn soon." you say. You hope it's true.

You spend the next few days imagining the questions you might be asked. Four days later, your name is called. It's time for your interrogation.

• Go to page 38.

You and two other men follow the guard out of the barracks. He leads you to the building where you had your health test. The interrogation room is small and crammed with furniture. You count two tables and five chairs. Two men at the bigger table wait for you to sit down. The guard who brought you in sits behind you. In the other corner of the room, a woman sits at a typewriter, ready to record everything that is said.

A big bald man speaks first. You don't understand him. The other man with glasses speaks in Chinese.

"Just tell the truth," he says.

You nod and take a deep breath. His questions come at you fast:

"Where is your village?"

"How many stories does your house have?"

"How many chickens do you have?"

"Are your mother's feet bound or unbound?"

"Where is the rice bin in your house?"

You don't have time to think. Luckily, you're able to answer truthfully and confidently.

"You seem very sure of your answers," the man says. "Did someone coach you?"

Your heart skips a beat. "No, sir," you say.

The bald man mumbles something to the other man, and the guard stands. You don't understand what they're saying. Then the guard taps you on the shoulder and signals for you to follow him out.

Your legs shake all the way back to the barracks. What's going to happen next?

Turn the page.

Barracks at Angel Island

When you get to your bunk bed, the guard says the only words he knows in Chinese.

"Pack bags," he says. "Welcome to Gold Mountain!"

THE END

To follow another path, turn to page 12.
To learn more about the difficult history of Asians in America, turn to page 101.

You can't take the chance that you'll forget your answers. You stuff the papers in your jacket pocket.

You join Father on deck. It's packed with people. Men in suits and big hats walk around checking papers. They release some of the passengers. The officials direct the rest of you to a smaller boat.

"This ferry is taking us to Angel Island," Father says. "That's where we'll be questioned and tested."

When you reach Angel Island, the immigrants are separated into groups. Suddenly, someone taps you on the shoulder. It's a tall man with a broad moustache. He says something you don't understand. Father's face turns pale.

"I told you to get rid of them," Father scolds.

Turn the page.

The tall man points to your jacket. There's a bulge where you hid the papers. Your lower lip quivers as he approaches you.

The man pulls out your papers and hands them to another man. You burst into tears. Both the man and your father shake their heads. You've never been more ashamed.

"How could you be so stupid?" Father demands.

You can't stop crying long enough to answer him. What will happen to you now?

Father walks up to the men and speaks to them. You don't understand what they're saying, but there's a lot of head shaking going on.

It feels like forever before Father returns. Sweat runs down the side of his face, which is now bright red.

Before he can explain what's happened, the big men shove the two of you back onto the ferry.

"They're sending us back to China," Father says through gritted teeth.

Your heart sinks. You have failed your family.

THE END

To follow another path, turn to page 12.
To learn more about the difficult history of Asians in America, turn to page 101.

CHAPTER 3

A NEW BRIDE'S ORDEAL

You're a 15-year-old girl. You live with your parents on a farm in Japan. You've never left home, but you dream of seeing the world.

One day, your parents tell you it's time for you to marry. You are going to be a "picture bride," like many of your friends before you. Your parents have chosen a husband for you, having only seen a picture of the man. As their daughter, it's your duty to obey.

Turn the page.

The idea scares you, but this is the way things are. Your husband-to-be lives in America. In his photo, he wears a fancy western suit. Your parents sent him a photo of you, and he has agreed to the match.

A young Japanese woman, late 1800s

Within the month, a wedding ceremony is performed. It's like any other wedding, with one notable difference—the groom isn't there. His parents and his photograph represent him. Once the ceremony is over, you leave home to go live with your parents-in-law. You stay with them until your husband sends for you.

You stay on your in-laws' farm, helping out like you did at home. You wait for your new husband to send you a ticket to travel. Soon, it's time to leave for America.

You pack your best kimono and board a giant ship. Your husband could only afford a third-class ticket. You spend a month at the bottom level of the ship, in the same corner as several other Japanese picture brides. Some are nervous, and others are excited. You show each other photos of your husbands.

Turn the page.

On the day the ship lands in San Francisco, you comb your hair and put on your silk kimono. You go up on deck and watch first-class passengers get off the ship. You clutch your passport and your bags and get ready to do the same.

"No such luck," an older woman tells you. "We're in third class. We have to go to Angel Island first."

What is Angel Island, you wonder? When your ferry pulls up to the island, you see white buildings and lots of flowering bushes and trees. It's a pretty place.

Just beyond the dock, there's a line of well-dressed men. They stare eagerly at the passengers coming off the ferry. You pull out the photo of your husband, just as all the other picture brides do. As you walk off the ship, you search for the face that matches your photo.

Asian immigrants arriving at Angel Island

Your heart sinks. Your husband looks much older than the photo you have. His hair is greying, and he has a wrinkled face. For the first time since the match, you aren't sure you can go through with it. What do you do?

- To refuse to be his wife, turn to page 50.
- To move on to the next step in the immigration process, turn to page 53.

You can't imagine spending your life with such an old man. Your first instinct is to run away. It would bring terrible dishonor to your family, but maybe your parents will understand and forgive you. *No*, you realize. *They wouldn't.*

Your heart is pounding a mile a minute. Suddenly, you find it hard to breathe. Your vision seems to go fuzzy, and then you faint.

When you wake, you're lying on a bed surrounded by strange women in white uniforms. They're speaking a language you don't understand. A woman in a dark dress speaks Japanese to you.

"I'm Fuku-san," she says. "You fainted when you arrived. You'll be fine after you eat."

"I want to go home," you cry. "My husband is so old. I cannot stay with an old man."

Fuku-san leans in and whispers. "If you really want to go home, you can 'accidentally' tell the interrogators that you're not who your papers say you are. Just know that you will never be able to come back."

Because you've been in the hospital for the day, you've already been examined and pass the health test. And you've had time to think about what you want to do.

- To lie and go home, turn to page 56.
- To accept your marriage and tell the truth, turn to page 63.

Picture brides arriving at Angel Island

The women on the ferry are separated from the male passengers. You all walk up to the large staircase beneath the big white building. There, the picture brides are allowed to meet their husbands for the first time.

The man who is your husband is called Hiro. He speaks gently and offers you some lovely, sweet buns. After the terrible ship food, this is a most welcome surprise.

"At least he's a gentleman, though he is older than my father," you think.

After a few minutes, guards arrive and usher the brides away.

"It's all right," Hiro says. "They're taking you to the hospital. You'll be examined for illness. Then they'll let you come home with me."

Turn the page.

The medical examination is humiliating. All the women are crammed inside a room with nurses in white uniforms. One of them speaks Japanese. She orders everyone to strip down to your underclothes. You've never done that in front of anyone, much less strangers.

To make things worse, the nurses ask you to do your bathroom business in a large bowl. They are testing it for diseases. The girl next to you is sobbing.

"I will fail this test," the girl beside you says. "The doctor back home said I had hookworm. If I do, they'll send me home."

This gives you an idea. Your parents would have to let you come home if you were too sick to stay in America.

"Switch bowls with me," you say.

The girl doesn't argue.

You fail your health test because they found worms in your sample. You're sent to the hospital for a few days. You are given medicine, and when the doctors test you again, you have no worms. Now you're afraid you'll have to go to live with your husband instead of being sent home.

You were never ill in the first place, but the hospital is filled with other sick people. Diseases spread quickly. The next day, your eyelid swells, just like the person in the bed next to you. You've caught their illness. It's called trachoma. This is a disease that means you have to be sent home.

Your plan has worked after all! But it was a gamble not worth taking. On the ship home, you become more ill. You die before seeing Japan again.

THE END

To follow another path, turn to page 12.
To learn more about the difficult history of
Asians in America, turn to page 101.

Fuku-san requests that you be interrogated immediately before leaving the hospital. She must have influence because the officials agree. She says she will interpret for you.

You are taken to a small room. Two men sit behind a table. They motion for you to sit on the other side. Your heart thumps nervously in your chest as you sit down. The men fire questions at you. Fuku-san repeats them in Japanese.

You've decided to lie. You burst into real tears and tell Fuku-san that the bride in the photo is your sister. She didn't want to leave Japan, so you took her place. Fuku-san repeats what you've said in English. The men frown at your answers. You can't tell it they're disappointed in your answer or if they don't believe you.

"Please forgive me," you say, hoping they believe you. "I will return home and never come back again."

The men talk to each other quietly. Then they call Hiro in. They tell him what's happened. When you see the sadness in his eyes, you feel awful. He knows you don't have a sister. You're both standing in front of the officials as they discuss in English what to do.

You and your husband look at each other while the white men discuss their decision. You can tell he wants to discuss the situation with you. But what will you say to him? Is your pity for him enough to make you stay? Or do you explain why you cannot be his wife?

• To reject your husband, turn to page 58.
• To give in to the pity you feel for him, turn to page 61.

"You're lying," Hiro whispers. "You don't have a sister."

"If you don't let me go home, I will run away," you threaten quietly.

"What will you do? You can't go home in disgrace?" his whisper grows louder.

A picture bride and her husband with officials at Angel Island

"Please don't talk to each other," the officials snap.

Hiro sighs deeply. It almost breaks your heart. He speaks in English to the men. Soon, everyone is shaking their heads. Has he given you away?

Fuku-san speaks to you. "He's agreed to let you go. You'll be on the next ship back to Japan."

Even though this is what you wanted, you're not sure you've made the right decision.

A ferry takes you back to the San Francisco port where you will get on a ship. You're very nervous. Will your family take you back in such disgrace?

With each passing day, you become more afraid that your parents won't take you back. You may be homeless when you reach Japan.

Turn the page.

In the large steerage room, you overhear others talking. Some are Japanese and are going to Hawaii. There are many immigrants there. There is work available on the sugar plantations.

This gives you an idea. You get off the ship in Hawaii. You tell the authorities that you are here to work on the plantations. You are allowed to stay.

You make your new life working in the sugar plantations in Hawaii. You never hear from your family again. You wonder what they think happened to you, but you're too afraid to reach out.

THE END

To follow another path, turn to page 12.
To learn more about the difficult history of Asians in America, turn to page 101.

As you and Hiro wait for the officials to finish their discussion, you struggle with your feelings. On the one hand, you can't imagine being married to such an old man. On the other hand, you must trust that your parents did what was best for you. And you've already lived with his parents for a year. You're a part of their family now. As hard as it is, you accept your fate.

"Please tell them I lied," you whisper. "It was fear that made me say those things."

Hiro's eyes widen. "You want to stay?"

"Quiet!" snaps an official.

Your husband speaks in English to the interrogator. You hope they accept your story. Soon, they stop speaking and Hiro turns to you.

"They will let you stay," he says. "I told them you are young and foolish."

Turn the page.

The officials ask you a few more questions. They sign some papers and hand them to Hiro. You leave with him.

On the ferry to San Francisco, you shiver. Hiro gives you his coat.

"I know you're scared," he says. "But I promise to take good care of you. I have a small business outside the city. We'll have a comfortable life."

Hiro sounds like a good man. You do your best to smile at his words.

As the city comes into view, you feel a little better. This is the beginning of a new adventure, just as you've always wanted.

"Welcome to America," he says as you step off the ferry to face your new life.

THE END

To follow another path, turn to page 12.
To learn more about the difficult history of Asians in America, turn to page 101.

You want to cry and run away. But you made a promise. You must keep your word.

When you leave the hospital, the officials let you meet with your husband for a few minutes.

"Call me Hiro." He speaks gently and offers you some delicious, sweet buns. You are hungry and grateful.

Hiro tells you about his home. He has a small shop in a nearby town. He's excited about having you help him in his business. He offers to teach you English too.

The more he speaks, the more comfortable you feel. He appears to be a good, kind man. Maybe life with him will be good.

Soon, the guards round up the women. You are told to follow them. This scares you.

Turn the page.

Asian women and children waiting to be processed at Angel Island

"They're going to be examined by the doctors," he says, "You've already passed your health test, but you still have your interrogation. Once that's done, they'll let you come home with me. It might take a day or two."

After the health tests are done, you and the women are taken across the lawn to another building. Men are led upstairs, while you and the women go into a large room on the ground floor.

There's nothing but rows and rows of bunk beds, three levels high. You find a third-level bunk and place your bag on the bed. There's a shared washroom and another room that has books and sewing materials in it.

There are women from many Asian countries on this floor. You hear them say that the European women stay in a different building.

Turn the page.

The white women get to leave Angel Island within a day or two, whereas the Asian women stay longer. The Chinese stay the longest.

"Just behave yourself, and don't lose your identification papers," an older Japanese woman says to you. "You'll be interrogated soon, and you'll need them to prove who you are."

That night, the guard announces that the next two days are holidays. None of the officials will be working. You're stuck here for at least three more days.

You hear women crying in the night.

"Why are we treated like prisoners?" someone whispers in the dark.

"I've been here for weeks," another voice adds. "I don't know if I can take this much longer."

As you try to sleep, you wonder if this is what life in America will be like. Will America feel like a big prison to you?

A little voice inside you whispers, "Being sent home may be a dishonor, but at least you can blame the authorities here. Would anyone blame you if somehow your identification papers got "lost." This is your last chance to go home. Do you take it?"

- To throw away your papers, turn to page 68.
- To keep your documents safe, turn to page 70.

Several days later, a guard orders everyone to the dining hall. You stuff your papers under your blouse and tell the guard you need to use the bathroom.

"Hurry up," he snaps.

Your heart pounds as you rip the documents up and throw them in the toilet. Hiro seems like a good man, but you can't imagine living the rest of your life in a country that treats you so badly.

The next two days go by very slowly. For most of the day, there's nothing to do but stare out the barred windows. In the afternoon, an American lady named Miss Kate and Fuku-san teach you a few phrases in English. It's a difficult language, but you're glad to have something to do aside from sewing.

Miss Kate seems kind. You wonder if perhaps you were wrong about the people here.

On the third day, interrogations begin again. You're called up late in the afternoon. When the officials realize you don't have any papers, there's a lot of head shaking and whispering. You're certain they'll put you on the next ship back to Japan. Have you made the wrong decision? Will your parents even take you back?

Hiro is called into the room. You watch as the expression on his face changes from anxious, to puzzled, and then to disappointment. He speaks English, and the conversation between him and the officials goes on for a long time. Finally, they stop talking.

"What will happen to me?" you ask Hiro.

He looks at you with kindness. "Luckily, I have copies of all your documents. They've agreed to let you come home with me."

• Go to page 73.

You search your small suitcase. Your identification papers are underneath your kimono. You spend the whole day looking through your papers, wondering if you have the courage to go through with your promise to be a good wife.

That night, the guards take all the women to the dining hall, a room with rows of long, wooden tables. In the middle of the table, there's a large bowl of rice with small fish and a few vegetables mixed together. The disgusting mixture reminds you of the slop you feed the pigs back home.

The food tastes terrible, but you're hungry, so you eat quickly. You wonder if the cooks even know how to make Asian food.

After dinner, the women are sent to a small fenced-in garden. You're encouraged to walk about and take in the fresh air. If you didn't feel like a caged animal, you might have enjoyed the view of the ocean and the pretty trees.

You cry yourself to sleep that night, wondering why you're being treated like a prisoner. As you fall asleep, you hear the other women crying too.

Turn the page.

By the fourth day on Angel Island, you feel like you've been here forever. But the guard enters the room and calls your name along with some others. You take your papers and head to the white building. There, you meet with some stern-looking men. Only one speaks Japanese. They look at your passport and marriage license, and they question you.

"Where did you live in Japan?"

"Have you been married before?"

"To your knowledge, has your husband been married before?"

You answer the questions with confidence.

When they've asked all their questions, they bring Hiro into the room. He looks nervous, but he smiles at you. They ask him the same questions. Finally, they're done.

The main interrogator says, "I move to accept this application. We should admit her to the country if they promise to get married again under U.S. law."

You agree, and your husband does too. It turns out that Fuku-san is married to a pastor. He will perform the marriage ceremony once you've settled in.

As you leave Angel Island, you look back at the buildings. Then you face the water and see the outline of San Francisco in front of you. You take a deep breath and prepare to begin your new life in America.

THE END

To follow another path, turn to page 12.
To learn more about the difficult history of Asians in America, turn to page 101.

CHAPTER 4

THE LONG WAIT

The snores of your neighboring detainees fill the stale air of the barracks. Your mind wanders. You think about your wife in the women's barracks. You haven't seen each other in days. Finally, you sit up and pull the stick from under your thin mattress.

You begin to carve the wall behind your bunk. You're carving a poem. You've been stuck on Angel Island for 289 days. That's longer than any other man you know. You don't know why. The guards never call your name.

Turn the page.

木屋拘留幾十天
所因墨例致牽連
可惜英雄無用武
只聽鷄聲未笑狂
可恨英雄無用武
只聽鷄聲未笑狂

從今遠別此樓中
各位鄉君眾歡同
莫道其間容西武
話感王勁變如龍

A poem carved into the wall at Angel Island

When you first arrived, you thought you'd be out in a week or so. You passed your health test. You studied all the interrogation questions. You knew every answer so well, it may as well be the truth. You could easily pass for the son of your uncle Yung Li, a merchant in San Francisco.

Maybe the officials know the truth. You aren't really Yung Li's son. You're what's called a paper son. You are pretending to be his son so you can have a better life in America.

Now you feel like you might be stuck on this island prison for the rest of your life. Being sent back to China is beginning to sound good.

You take that back. Your parents and nine siblings back home are counting on you to succeed. You must send money back to them so they can afford to eat. Even your in-laws are hoping to benefit from your success in America.

Turn the page.

You're too sad to think of that now. You raise the stick to another section of the wall.

It feels like a thousand nights have passed
I thought I was coming to freedom
But instead, a prison is all I find.

The carving is slow going. You don't want the guards to know what you're up to, so you wait until everyone is asleep to carve. Then you cover it with the laundry hung off your bunk.

"Someday, someone will read this and know my pain," you say to yourself. "Maybe they'll find comfort in my words."

Creak! Thump!

What's that sound? Is it a guard or has someone fallen out of their bunks again?

Do you lie down or continue to carve?

- To ignore the sound and continue, go to the next page.
- To jump into bed, turn to page 81.

Someone's probably fallen out of bed. You continue to carve.

Thwap!

Something hard strikes the back of your head. A hand grabs your shirt and pulls you into the air. You hang there like a limp doll.

"What are you doing?" the guard demands. It's Mr. John, the guard with the short temper.

The men sleeping around you wake up, but no one moves. They don't dare interfere.

Mr. John drags you out of the barracks to the narrow hallway by the stairs. You glance down and see the door to the women's dormitory. You think of your wife's safety.

"Please sir, I'm sorry," you begin. Mr. John has been here so long that he speaks a bit of Chinese. You know he understands you.

Turn the page.

"I should report you," he says gruffly. "Send you back to China. What were you doing out of bed? Stealing your neighbor's belongings?"

He didn't see you carving!

"I was unable to sleep," you lie. "I needed to stretch my legs. I promise I wasn't stealing."

"I'm not interested in your promises," he says. "I must report you in the morning."

You fall to your knees and beg him. Then an idea occurs to you. You could try to bribe the guard. Will that get you into more trouble, or could it save you?

- To bribe the guard, turn to page 84.
- To keep begging for mercy, turn to page 88.

You can't take the risk of getting caught carving words into the wall. It's against the rules.

You jump back into bed and pretend to be asleep. When you hear footsteps, you hold your breath and thank the heavens that you did. One day soon, it'll be your turn to leave this awful place and enter America.

You decide you should get back to studying your notes as soon as breakfast is over tomorrow. But the very next morning you are called up for your interrogation. The officials fire questions so fast, you barely have time to think.

"Who are the elders in your village?"

"How many children does your neighbor on the right have?"

"Where is the rice bin kept in your house?"

Turn the page.

An Asian immigrant being
interrogated at Angel Island, 1931

You have a good memory, and even though you haven't read your notes in days, you remember all the answers. You reply with confidence.

Finally, the officials nod their heads and sign a piece of paper. They hand it to you and say, "Welcome to America, Mr. Yung."

Your wife is called in for the interrogation after you. An hour later, she emerges from the room with a relieved smile. She has passed too.

By the end of the day, you and your wife are taking the ferry across the water to San Francisco. Yung Li waits for you. He's happy to have someone to help him in his business, and you're glad to finally have made it to the Gold Mountain.

THE END

To follow another path, turn to page 12.
To learn more about the difficult history of
Asians in America, turn to page 101.

You swallow your fear and take a risk.

"If you let this pass, I can pay you," you say.

Mr. John laughs. "Pay me? With what? Peanuts? Rice?"

"I have a pearl," you say. "My mother gave it to me. It was my grandmother's."

The guard glares at you. "You should have declared all valuables when you arrived," he says in a low, warning voice. "If you lied about that, you could be lying about being a true son. I should definitely report you."

"Please don't. Wouldn't you rather have a lovely pearl for yourself?"

"Where is this pearl?" he asks.

"In my luggage, in the baggage shed," you say

Will his greed be enough to save you tonight?

"Fine," Mr. John says. "Tomorrow is a walk day. When we go to the baggage shed, you will bring me the pearl."

"Thank you, sir," you say with relief. Your hands are shaking.

The guard sends you back to bed, but you can't sleep the rest of the night. That pearl was a wedding gift to your mother. She gave it to your wife on your wedding day. It's the only thing of value that you have.

The next day, you skip breakfast. The food is barely edible anyway.

During the walk, the men are let out into a courtyard that is surrounded by sharp, barbed wire fences. The guards escort a few men at a time to the baggage shed to get extra clothes or books. You go with Mr. John.

Turn the page.

You hate that he'll get your wife's pearl. But you have to do everything you can to make it through Angel Island.

You pull a jacket from your small suitcase and hand it to him. He rips the hem and pulls out a shiny, white pearl. He examines it with a greedy look in his eyes. Your heart sinks as you watch him revel in your precious family heirloom.

"This will make a fine gift," he says.

You sigh in relief and expect him to walk you back to the barracks. Instead, he looks down at your suitcase.

"What else do you have hiding in here?" he asks. He rummages through your things. Your heart stops when he pulls out a small photograph of you with your real parents. Your mother must have put it in your suitcase.

Mr. John takes the photograph and turns it over to his supervisor. The supervisor goes through your papers and decides that you have been lying to them. You are a paper son, as they had suspected. Now they have their proof.

Your sobbing wife is brought to your side. Both of you are put onto a ship. You're going back to China, with no money, and no hope.

THE END

To follow another path, turn to page 12.
To learn more about the difficult history of Asians in America, turn to page 101.

You beg Mr. John for mercy. He huffs. I'll let this slide if you do something for me."

This sounds dangerous, but you nod, afraid to refuse.

"I will let you go this one time, if you tell me who in your barracks are the paper sons."

Your legs go weak. You are a paper son. How can you betray others who, like you, are trying to make a better life for themselves?

When you don't say anything, Mr. John says. "Get back to bed immediately. In two nights, I will come back at midnight, and you will give me at least three names. If not, I will report your behavior to my supervisor."

You toss and turn for the rest of the night. What will you do?

To refuse to betray others, go to the next page.
To turn in three other men, turn to page 97.

You cannot betray these men. They're your friends. You came over with many of them on the ship in steerage. They've helped you study for your interrogation. They're keeping your secret as much as you're keeping theirs. You cannot turn them in.

Chinese immigrants in steerage

Turn the page.

Two nights later, when you meet Mr. John, you tell him you have no names for him. You hope he has a heart. But in case he doesn't, you've retrieved some insurance from your bag in the storage shed. It's a pearl your mother gave your wife as a wedding gift.

Mr. John's face turns a bright red. He brings his whistle up to his lips. You put out a hand to stop him from alerting the other guards.

"I have something better than paper sons," you say.

He pauses, curious to hear more. You show him the pearl.

"Sounds like something we could agree on," he says.

You hand over the only precious thing you have from home. Mr. John keeps his word and doesn't report you.

You continue to while away the days on Angel Island. In the daytime, you listen to old records in the day room with the other men. Sometimes, you play chess or read a book.

Each night, you get up and continue to carve your poem into the wall. Mr. John doesn't bother you anymore.

Finally, on day 312, your name is called! You slip your coaching book to a friend, who will destroy the pages. You've done this for others.

A new guard walks you and three others out of the barracks toward the main building. You sit on a bench in a hallway while the first man goes in for the test. It feels like a very long time has passed before he emerges again. When he does, he is grinning.

"I passed!" he whispers to you.

Turn the page.

You congratulate him, but your heart is thumping loudly. Will you have the same success?

You're led into a small room. Three men sit around a table. You sit in the chair across from them. Behind you, a woman is typing every word that is said.

A vintage typewriter

A bald man fires questions at you. Having been here for more than 300 days, you understand a few of his words, but not enough to answer with confidence. Luckily, there's an interpreter.

"How long have you been married?"

"How many steps are there from the back of your house to the front door?"

"Where does your family store their rice?"

The questions come at you fast, but you're prepared. You've had almost a year to study them.

When the interrogator stops, his brows are knitted tightly together. He mumbles something to the interpreter, but the question isn't translated to you. They talk for a long time.

Turn the page.

The door to the room opens, and your wife walks in. She looks thinner and paler than when you left China. She stares at the men, nervously. You want to speak to her, but the guards shush you.

You stand in a corner of the room as the interrogator asks her the same questions.

She must have studied as hard as you did because she answers the questions easily. With each answer, the interrogator looks over at you, as if he's trying to read your mind. You hope that you and your wife aren't answering too quickly to be suspicious.

It feels like hours later when the questioning ends. The door to the room opens one more time. In walks a Chinese gentleman dressed in a very nice American suit. You recognize him from the photograph in your coaching book. Mr. Yung.

"Father!" you say, hoping it's a convincing act.

Mr. Yung smiles at you. He looks a little uncomfortable.

The interrogator asks Mr. Yung a few questions. Mr. Yung answers in fluent English. Finally, the interrogator picks up his pen and signs a piece of paper. He hands gestures to Mr. Yung.

"Welcome to America," Mr. Yung says to you. He looks as relieved as you feel.

"Thank you, father," you reply.

You let out the breath you were holding, and your wife begins to cry. You take her by the arm and bow to the interrogator and the interpreter.

"Thank you, thank you," you say in English.

Turn the page.

Mr. Yung helps to carry your luggage. As you walk over the bridge toward the ferry that will take you to San Francisco, you stop and take one last look behind you. You think of the friends who are still here, and the poem you've carved for the men who have yet to arrive. You are so glad to be leaving. You never want to see Angel Island again.

THE END

To follow another path, turn to page 12.
To learn more about the difficult history of Asians in America, turn to page 101.

You toss and turn all night. You know who the paper sons are. You've helped them memorize their papers, just as they've helped you. They've become your friends. And you know that none of you can return to China empty-handed without letting a lot of people down.

But you must think of your own family too. Your wife is counting on you to get both of you into San Francisco. If you fail, she does too. And if you both fail, your families will starve. You have no choice.

Two nights later, you give the names of three men who are paper sons to Mr. John. You feel sick doing it.

The decision backfires. When the three men are exposed for being paper sons, they realize that someone has betrayed them. One of them gives up more names—including yours.

Turn the page.

You and your wife are sent away immediately. The two of you end up back in Hong Kong. You are too ashamed to go to your home village. Your wife is furious with you.

You and your wife spend the rest of your days struggling to make ends meet. You find whatever work you can. You send your meager savings back home. You doubt it is enough.

THE END

To follow another path, turn to page 12.
To learn more about the difficult history of
Asians in America, turn to page 101.

CHAPTER 5

THE DIFFICULT HISTORY OF ASIANS IN AMERICA

In the mid-1800's, hundreds of thousands of Chinese immigrants came to America. They fled wars and famine. Most of them were men. They worked as miners or built the railroads. They worked hard for low wages, sending most of that money back to their families in China.

Turn the page.

White Americans became angry, believing that the Chinese were taking their jobs. Violent attacks against the Chinese grew. In 1882, the U.S. government passed a law. It was called the Chinese Exclusion Act. It was the first law ever to exclude a particular race of people from coming to America.

When the Chinese were stopped from immigrating, there weren't enough cheap workers in America. Japanese immigrants were willing to take these jobs. They too worked in factories, on railroads, and in mines. Many worked on farms in California or sugar plantations in Hawaii.

Again, white Americans grew angry. More laws were passed to keep the number of Japanese immigrants low. Men could, under strict rules, bring wives to America. This is how picture brides came to be.

Chinese immigrants working to build the transcontinental railroad

From 1910 to 1940, up to 1 million immigrants passed through Angel Island. The Chinese Exclusion Act finally ended in 1943. That's when the U.S. needed China to help them in World War II (1939–1945).

During World War II, Angel Island was used to hold prisoners of war. For a while, it also held American citizens. When Japan attacked Pearl Harbor in Hawaii, the U.S. government suspected Japanese Americans might be disloyal. They imprisoned many Japanese Americans. It was a dark time in U.S. history.

Years later, the California Department of Parks and Recreation turned Angel Island into a park. They prepared to tear down the crumbled buildings. But, in 1970, park ranger Alexander Weiss found carvings of poetry in the walls of the barracks. Most were in Chinese, but others were in Japanese and other languages.

Historians fought to turn these buildings into a museum. Today, people can go there to learn about the suffering of those held there. The museum shines a light on how difficult life was for Asian immigrants. It keeps their stories alive.

The Chinese Exclusion Act

Angel Island Immigration Station Timeline

January 24, 1848
Gold is discovered at Sutter's Mill in California. Gold fever draws people to California.

1870's
Economic downturn leads white people to lose jobs and begin to blame Asian immigrants for their suffering.

May 6, 1882
President Chester A. Arthur signs the Chinese Exclusion Act into law. It bars Chinese laborers from coming to the United States.

January 21, 1910
Angel Island Immigration Station opens to receive and process immigrants.

August 1940
Fire destroys the main administration building on Angel Island. The immigration station moves to the mainland.

December 7, 1941
Japan attacks the United States at Pearl Harbor. The U.S. enters World War II (1939–1945).

1942-1945
The U.S. military uses Angel Island to process prisoners of war and to detain hundreds of Japanese Americans.

1943
Congress repeals the Chinese Exclusion Act but limits Chinese immigration to only 105 people per year.

1946
The Army gives the Angel Island facility back to the state of California.

1963
The California Department of Parks and Recreation turns the abandoned Angel Island into a park.

1965
The Immigration and Nationality Act of 1965 is passed. It goes into effect July 1, 1968.

July 1, 1968
The Immigration Act allows a maximum of 170,000 non-Western immigrants to come to the United States.

1970
Park ranger Alexander Weiss discovers the carvings on the walls of the Angel Island buildings and stops their destruction.

1990
The Immigration Act of 1990 removes the caps on the non-Western immigrants.

1997
Angel Island Immigration Station is declared a National Historic Landmark.

March 8, 2022
Angel Island Hospital is restored and reopened as a museum.

Other Paths to Explore

1. Imagine growing up in a poor village in a country at war. Your only shot at a better life is lying about who you are to have a chance at a new life in a new country. Would you take that chance? Why or why not?

2. Imagine that your grandfather told you that your family name isn't what you've grown up with. What could you do to discover the truth about your ancestors? Would it be important to you? Why or why not?

3. Imagine you were a child arriving on Angel Island with your mother. There are no other children to play with, and no toys or games. Can you think of objects that you might find to create a game for yourself?

Bibliography

Chinese American: Exclusion/Inclusion/Paper Sons & Daughters
youtube.com/watch?v=2yzU_34oY8k

Heart Mountain: Coming to America Japanese
heartmountain.org/history/coming-to-america/

Lee, Erika and Yung, Judy. *Angel Island: Immigrant Gateway to America.*
New York: Oxford University Press, 2010.

Lai, Him Mark, Lim Genny, Yung, Judy. *Island: Poetry and History of Chinese Immigrants on Angel Island, 1920-1940.* Seattle: University of Washington Press, 2014.

Paper Sons: Chinese American Illegal Immigrants
youtube.com/watch?v=Hhc-om3SXKw

Glossary

barracks (BAR-uhks)—a building where detainees live for a short amount of time

citizenship (SI-tuh-zuhn-ship)—the state of being a citizen, which is a person who is a member of a country either because of being born there or being declared a member by law

deport (di-PORT)—to send people back to their own country

detainee (dee-tayn-EE)—a person who is held in custody, usually for questioning or political reasons, while not being a criminal

exclusion (eks-CLUE-zhun)—the act of keeping something or someone out

interrogation (in-tayr-uh-GAY-shun)—the process of questioning someone aggressively, especially a suspect, detainee, or prisoner

steerage (STEE-rij)—the least expensive place for passengers to travel in a ship; it was called steerage because it was located near the rudder, which helped steer the ship

Read More

Bybee, Veeda. *Li on Angel Island*. North Mankato, MN: Stone Arch Books, an imprint of Capstone, 2021.

Kim, Carol. *The Real History of Angel Island*. Minneapolis: Lerner Publications, 2023.

Loh-Hagan, Virginia. *Detained and Interrogated: Angel Island Immigration*. Ann Arbor, MI: Cherry Lake Publishing, 2020.

Internet Sites

Angel Island Immigration Station Foundation
aiisf.org

History.com: Angel Island Immigration Station
history.com/topics/immigration/angel-island-immigration-station

U.S. Immigration Station, Angel Island
nps.gov/places/u-s-immigration-station-angel-island.htm

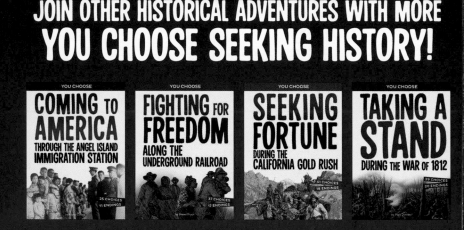
About the Author

Ailynn Collins has written many books for children, from stories about aliens and monsters, to books about science and nature, the past and the future. These are her favorite subjects. She has an MFA from Hamline University and was a teacher for many years. She mentors kids who love to write stories of their own. She lives outside Seattle with her family and 5 dogs. When she's not writing, she enjoys participating in dog shows and dog sports.